BUFFY

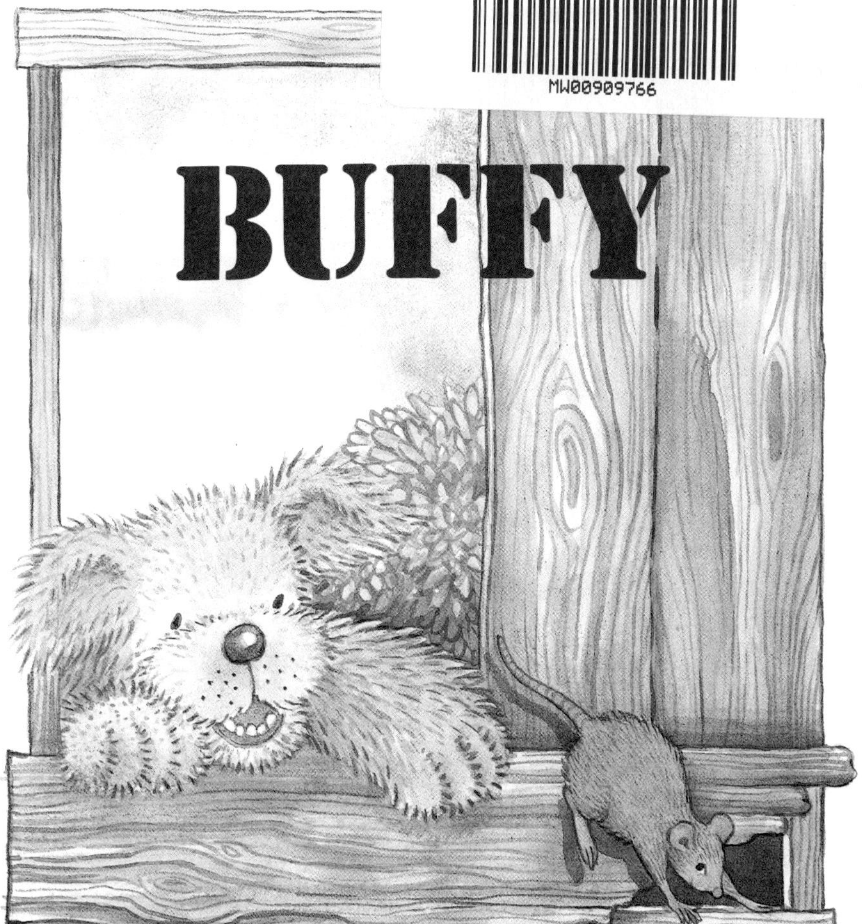

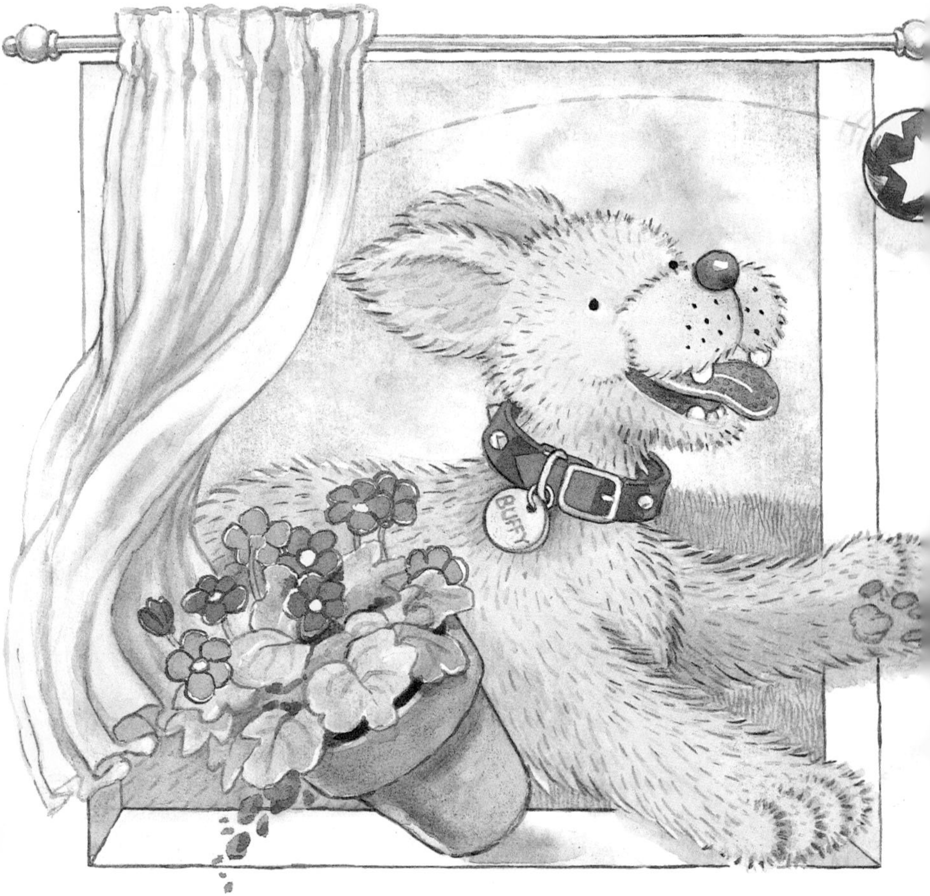

Buffy chased a ball.

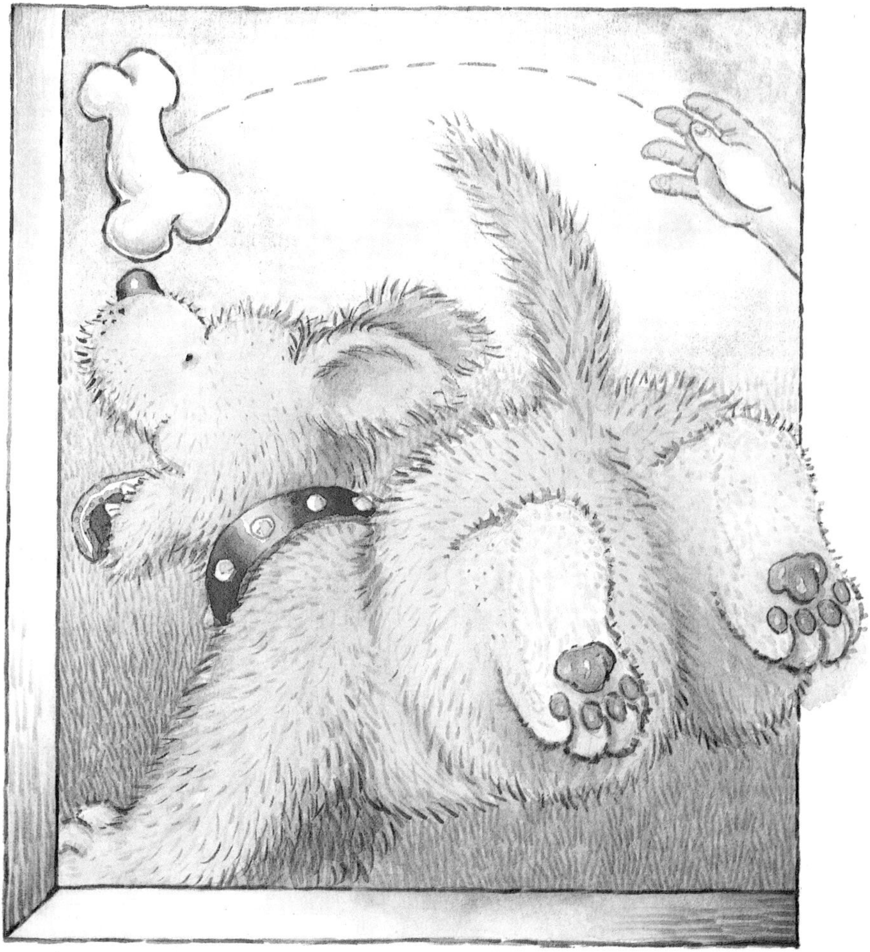

Buffy chased a bone.

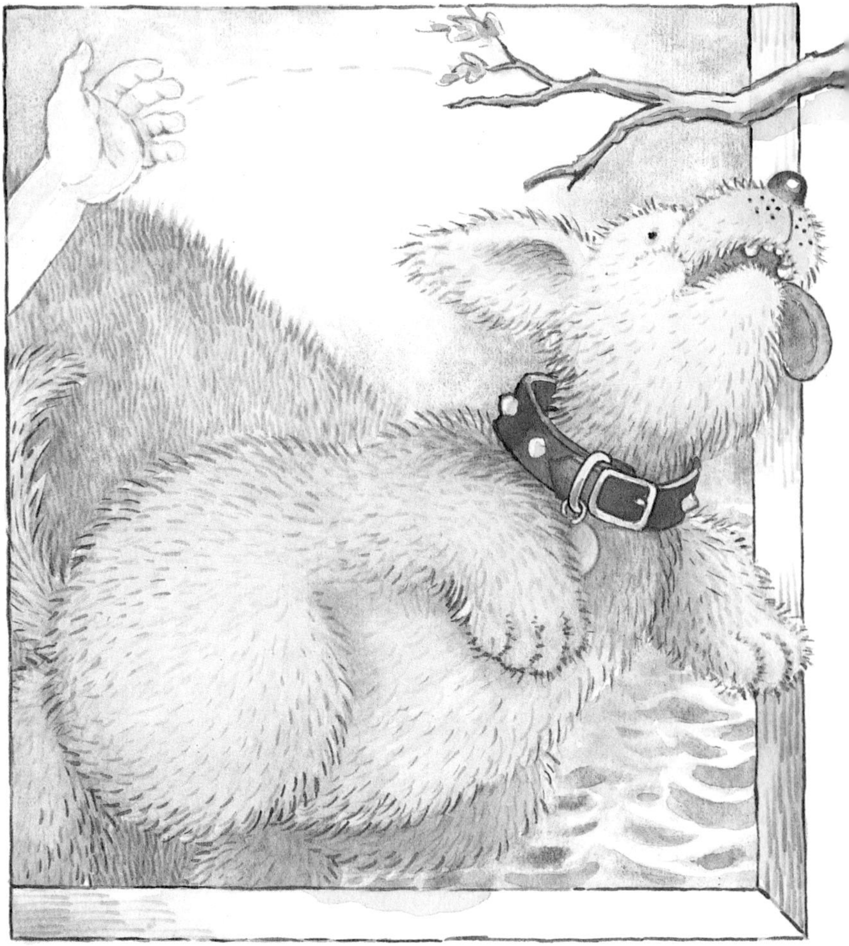

Buffy chased a stick.

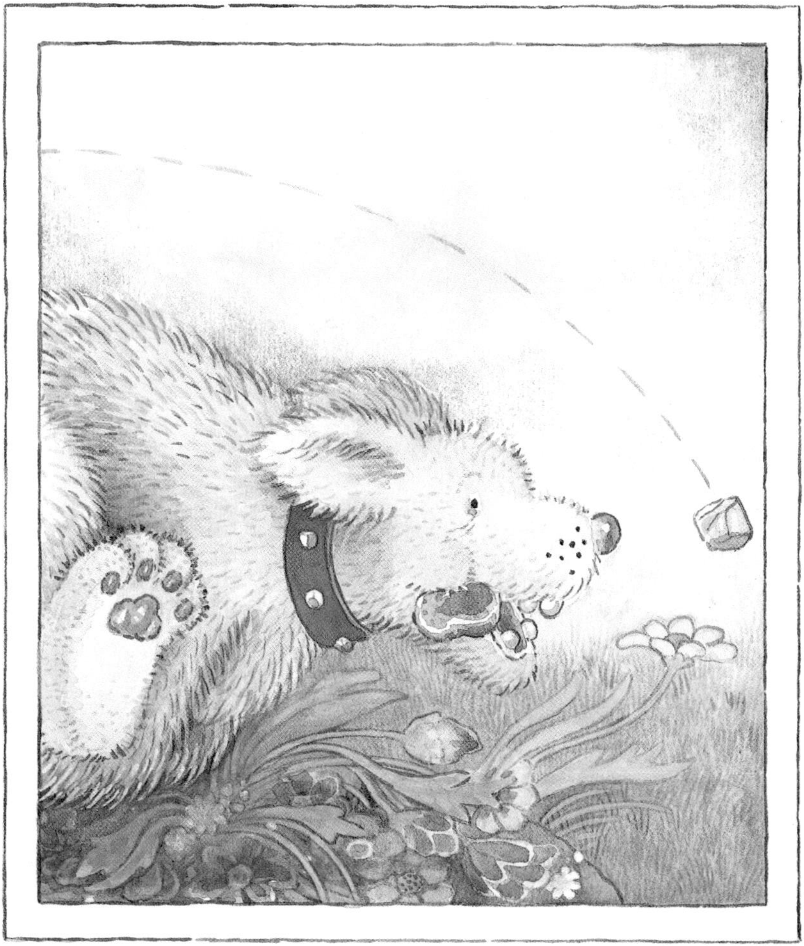

Buffy chased a stone.

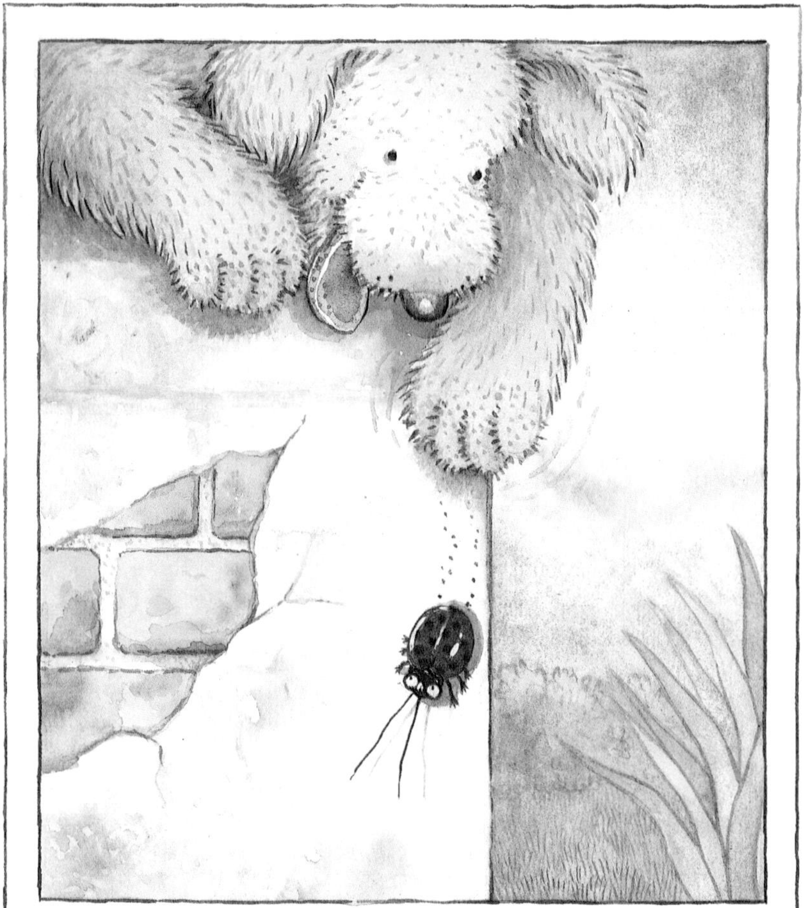

Buffy chased a bug.

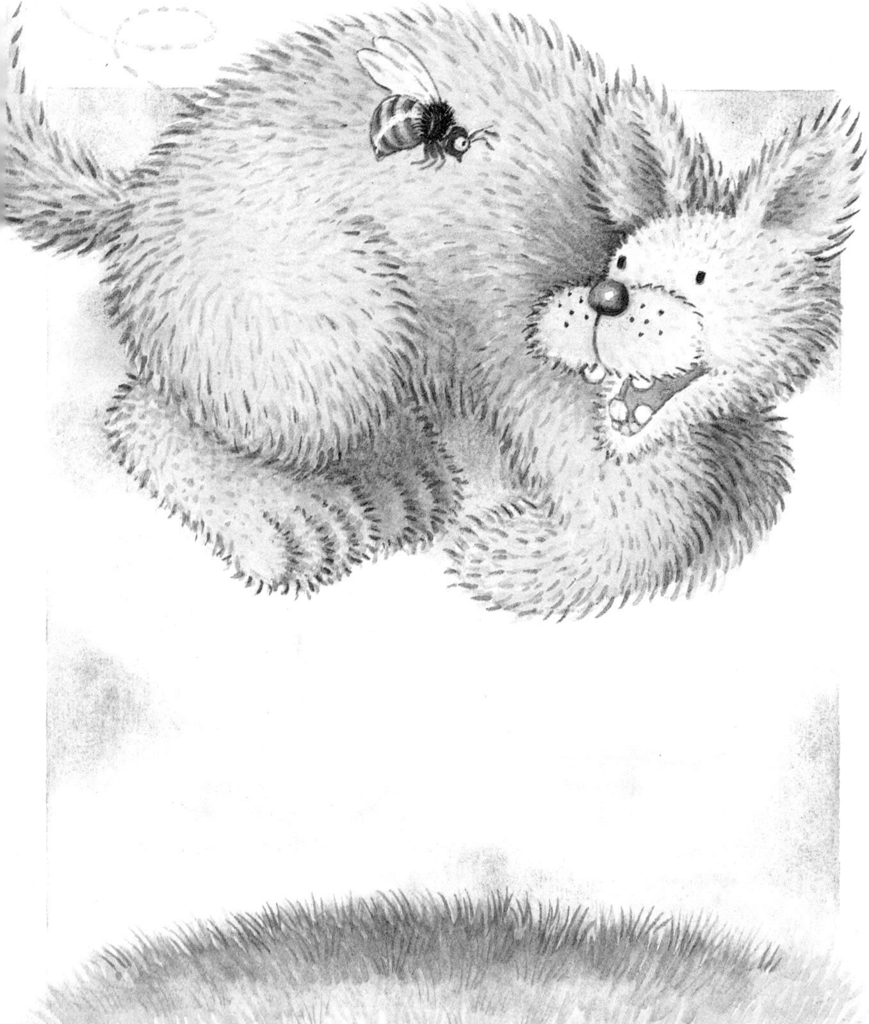

Buffy chased a bee.

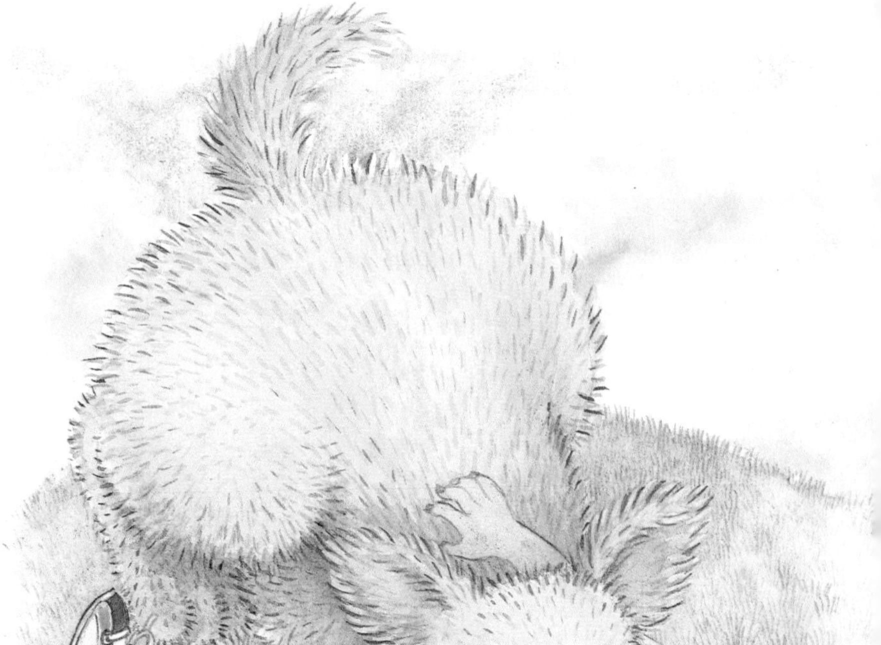

Buffy knocked me over –
Buffy caught *me*!